CW01476448

You Broke Up When
You Said "I Do"

How to Be A Better Wife and Make Your Husband
The Happiest Person In the World by Changing
These Behavioral Habits That Women Develop In
Long-Lasting Relationships

Martha B. Bailey

Bluesource And Friends

This book is brought to you by Bluesource And Friends, a happy book publishing company.

Our motto is **"Happiness Within Pages"**

We promise to deliver amazing value to readers with our books.

We also appreciate honest book reviews from our readers.

Connect with us on our Facebook page

www.facebook.com/bluesourceandfriends and stay tuned to our latest book promotions and free giveaways.

Don't forget to claim your FREE books!

Brain Teasers:

https://tinyurl.com/karenbrainteasers

Harry Potter Trivia:

https://tinyurl.com/wizardworldtrivia

Sherlock Puzzle Book (Volume 2)

https://tinyurl.com/Sherlockpuzzlebook2

Also check out our other books

"67 Lateral Thinking Puzzles"

https://tinyurl.com/thinkingandriddles

"Rookstorm Online Saga"

https://tinyurl.com/rookstorm

"Korman's Prayer"

https://tinyurl.com/kormanprayer

"The Convergence"

https://tinyurl.com/bloodcavefiction

"The Hardest Sudokos In Existence

(Ranked As The Hardest Sudoku Collection

Available In The Western World)"

https://tinyurl.com/MasakiSudoku

Table of Contents

You Broke Up When You Said "I Do"

Introduction

Thank you for choosing to read "*You Broke Up When You Said 'I Do'*". The purpose of this book is to try and point you in the right direction to make your marriage a successful one. Using some of the tips and tools provided in this book is not a guaranteed game changer when it comes to you and your relationship, but they should absolutely help you in times of need. As you read this book, you will learn how to give yourself and your spouse the freedom you both long deserve, and get yourself outside of your comfort zone.

Teach yourself not to think as an "I" but as a "we", and show your husband the respect and dignity that he is worthy of receiving. You will, hopefully, see yourself in a new light and understand how important it is that you recognize you who are as an individual before trying to please someone else. Understand your role as a parent and learn that the choices you make are mutual and should stay that way. Learn how you should stop criticizing and start praising your loved one, and also to stop criticizing yourself.

The way this book is meant to be read is not as, "What am I doing wrong?" But to stop and put yourself in the opposite position and start thinking, "How would I feel if they were doing this to me?" And "How could I take the opportunity to make this situation better?" I hope you will enjoy this book and take many great lessons with you.

Chapter 1

You found it once; you can find it again.

They say that the first five years of a relationship is the hardest. You either "make it" or you "break it". You experience so much as a couple in the first five years of a relationship and sometimes the struggles you face will be enough for you to realize that maybe this isn't exactly what you wanted, or you will realize that, "Hey, this person is the person I want to do life with".

When you first meet that person that gives you butterflies and makes you smile uncontrollably all the time for no reason, you are forever chasing to get that feeling again. After a while, you begin to submerge yourself in a feeling of comfort, and you get relaxed.

You Broke Up When You Said "I Do"

Little by little, you might start to not wear as much make-up, or you skip a couple days on shaving your legs. If you're not working, then your hair doesn't get done, and you don't bother to try to get all dressed up. You would rather stay home and watch TV than make the effort to get up and get out, because it's easier that way. You spend less money, and don't have to put forth effort to spend time with your significant other. Then, you wake up one day, asking yourself, "What the hell happened?"

Where is the love? Where is that attraction? When did we stop having fun together?

Well dear, it's still there. Somewhere, deep down, you have buried it—you both did. It's not your fault and it's not his—it's just life. We get so wrapped up in our day-to-day lives that we just kind of quit enjoying the thrill of the race—the race to your "happily ever after".

It's not a race, though. Love isn't something you just forget about once you reach the "finish line" of finally making it "official" that you're in a relationship. Hang it up on the shelf and give yourself a pat on the back. No, the finish line is when you're both eighty years old, sitting on your front porch in your rocking chairs, saying to yourselves, "We did it, we made it".

Don't wait around for things to change. It's your time to shine, and if you want things to be different, then you need to start NOW.

Put your face on!

Get up! Get dressed and go to the store. First and foremost, go buy yourself a new razor and some make-up. Keep in mind that the outcome for this is not sex! That will come later on and with time. Right now, you just need to remember the reason you fell in love with each other in the first place.

Take a little extra time in the morning for yourself, even if its just a little mascara or lip gloss. Men can be a little simple-minded sometimes when it comes to complimenting women, so don't just do it for your man. Take pride in yourself and your man will be sure to notice, but don't get upset or discouraged if nothing is said. If you're asked why you are "getting all dressed up", simply reply "I just felt like it". There is nothing wrong with trying to look good for yourself because, in turn, you are looking good for your man.

Sunshine and Smiles

It's infectious. When someone smiles at you, your automatic response is to smile back. If you hear laughter, it fills you up with joy on the inside. There is nothing better than being happy and content so show it! Most of us ladies are known for that awful "resting bitch face" or "RBF", and it really is our downfall. Everyone around you is always thinking that something is wrong or you are mad, sad, or anything

BUT happy, so it is time for you to make the conscious effort to turn that frown upside-down.

When trying to bring the spark back into your relationship, it's crucial to be optimistic. Your perceived "bad attitude" can alter your significant others attitude as well, and they could start the down-hill spiral of "What did I do now?" And that is something you do not want. Keep in mind that you both will play off each other's moods. If you're mad and upset, then your significant other will more than likely become the same way, espccially if they think that they are the one that caused you to be upset in the first place.

The point is, if you are happy, then you don't need to be shy about showing off those pearly whites of yours.

Explore

You Broke Up When You Said "I Do"

Grocery shopping, again? If quality time you spend with your spouse/significant other consists of just going to Walmart, then a change definitely needs to be made. Sure, it's fun making those late night runs to get some snacks and food, but as a couple, you need more than that.

It doesn't take much to have fun. Whether it's a walk on the beach or in a park, making some sandwiches and just having a picnic somewhere, you're looking for that quality time together. Take two hours out of an afternoon, get yourself all dolled-up, and just go. If you are having trouble figuring out what you should do or where to go, then you need to get your partner to sit with you and write down several places to go visit or eat, toss them all into a hat and mix them up really well, then pick one at random. This way, there is no argument on where to go or what to do.

You can also use this strategy for weeks and months to come.

Touch

We often time forget the power a physical touch has. A slight caress on the hand as you walk by or just a hug as soon as your significant other walks in the door from a long day at work—the smallest of things have the power to make us feel wanted.

Talk

A simple conversation can go a long way.

After a long day at work or at home with the kids, try to make the effort to sit down with your partner after you get settled for the night, and if you have kids, put them to bed. Light some candles, turn on some music and pour yourself a glass of wine and pull your spouse to the couch. You can start with small talk, sure, but try to bring up memories. Reminisce on "old times" and LAUGH together. This will bring you closer than you think, and you will go to bed with that warm fuzzy feeling.

Also, don't be afraid to ask questions. One of the biggest problems in relationships is communication. If your significant other is doing something that you don't like, then just ask them nicely to stop. They might not even realize they are doing something that makes you upset or uncomfortable.

Dance

There is nothing like being held in the arms of the person you love, even if you or your partner isn't a person who likes to dance. Step outside of your comfort zone and give yourself the chance to be a little vulnerable.

One afternoon, before your spouse gets home, clean the house and make sure that you are showered and dressed cute and comfortable (if you want go all out and doll yourself up, then that is fine too, but for this step, I want you to stay home instead of going out). Have dinner cooked, dim the lights, light some candles, and turn on some of your favorite slow tunes.

Be ready to give your man a kiss when he walks through the door; tell him to go shower and come back and find you. He will more than likely be skeptical at this point, but don't let it deter you from your end goal—being in his arms.

Once he is out of the shower, dressed, and in your line of sight, turn up the music and pull him to you. If he starts back-peddling, tell him to stop and just enjoy the moment. It doesn't matter if he can't dance, or if you are shy—all you have to do is sway around the room in each other's arms. Once you succeed in having your moment, sit down together and enjoy your dinner.

Chances are, you have been building each other up from the moment you started this, and tension should be running high right about now, but definitely in a good way. Take a chance and see where the moment takes you.

Kids

You love them, but don't talk about them.

Every conversation you have with your spouse does not have to pertain to your children. It is important to find some distance between you and your children when you are trying to rekindle the love in your relationship.

Checking in

During the day when you are separated, call your spouse on his lunch break or send him a short email just to let him know that you are thinking about him.

Texting

Texting your spouse can be fun and flirty if you let it. Since you both probably don't have a lot of time between working and taking care of kids and a household, texting is an easy way for you to flirt during those busy hours of the day.

Start by sending him a selfie and adding a "kissy face" emoji and tell him that you are thinking about him.

Don't be scared to take things a little further and be a little naughty. Text him and tell him that you can't stop thinking about him and his touch. Tell him to come home early and you will be waiting for him. Say things to him that will make him blush, for example, what you want to do to him later that night when you go bed.

Think "promiscuous" when you text him.

Of course, there is always a time and place for naughty texting, or "sexting", also able to be done through some encouraging, simple and sweet texts as well.

Mind Reading

When trying to find that common ground again in your relationship, don't try to read his mind. You more than likely don't know what he is thinking, so try not act like you do, because feelings will end up hurt.

Role Playing

There are several meanings of the term "role playing", so you can pick your poison when it comes to this topic. Start small though and build yourself up to a bigger work of art. Think about one of your first dates and pick your favorite one. When I say "first", I mean the first one to five dates, and whichever one you decide you like the best or was your favorite, reenact it. Take yourselves back in time when you gave each other butterflies and smiles.

I Wish I May, I Wish I Might

Once you are well on your way to finding that spark again within your relationship, grab a pen and a piece of paper, crawl into bed with some snacks, and start making a "sex list". Write down all the things you want to try and what you are adamant on not trying, start telling all your dirty little secrets. What are your fantasies and your obsessions? What are things that turn you on the most, and what are things that don't turn you on? What do you want to do your spouse and, most importantly, what do you want him to do to you?

This can also be an embarrassing moment for you, but just keep on talking through it. It is important for you to satisfy your partner and for your partner to know how to please you.

Curiosity Killed the Cat

Spice it up by throwing in some surprises here and there. Whether it is for something fun or romantic, try new things and learn how to be mysterious.

Massages

Spend a whole night doing nothing but giving each other full body massages! This is a fun and relaxing way to get the blood flowing, and hormones rising. It can be used as a great source of foreplay and it also gets your mind and body at ease.

You Broke Up When You Said "I Do"

Trying to find the spark in your relationship again can sometimes be a difficult task to tackle, but with some dedication and patience, you can surely succeed in your endeavors.

Chapter 2

Motherhood is one of the most satisfying, terrifying and rewarding things you could ever encounter. You spent nine months forming a tiny human in your belly, and you haven't slowed down since the day you came home from the hospital with the small bundle of joy. Every tear shed, every bottle made, every diaper changed, every tantrum witnessed and those sleepless nights—you wouldn't trade it for the world. You look into those tiny eyes, and they are filled with an endless amount of love, and to them, you can do no wrong—you are their everything— their life source.

There's something to be said about a mother's love, and yet words can never fully express just what a mother feels. Sure, you wouldn't trade it for the world, but is it too much to shower in peace? Having a meal where tiny fingers are not picking away at your plate or even do laundry without having to continuously re-fold clothes because your little monsters want to "help", only to feel guilty when you do finally get that moment of peace.

As mothers, we're constantly fighting a never-ending battle that our spouses just don't understand, and there is always something running through our minds. We wake up, make sure the kids are fed, bathed and clothed. The house is destroyed and put back together all before 10 am.

One of the biggest challenges I think that women face is the feeling of equality when it comes to the subject of "who does more" between you and your spouse. When you are a stay-at-home mom, most days, you just don't get the luxury of sitting around binge-watching your favorite T.V show, especially when you have children of small ages. You're constantly moving around, picking up after the tiny humans, feeding them, playing with them, and being their shoulder to cry on, and the list goes on and on.

Our little ones don't quite know how to show us the appreciation we deserve, and who can blame them? Of course, you recognize that your spouse does their duty by supporting your household and going to work every day and "busting their butts", but more often than not, as stay-at-home mothers, you tend to get the cold shoulder because all you do is "sit at home". It doesn't matter how much you get done, because it's expected of you to have a clean home, laundry done and dinner done by the time your significant others arrives home.

Is it too much to ask for a little appreciation? A simple "thank you" can go a long way.

Make sure to remember that as well when it comes to your spouse. Although you may feel unappreciated, your significant other could be feeling the same way, so when you know that they have had a long day at work, even though your day has been long too, be sure that you show your appreciation for your loved one as well.

Sometimes, you get wrapped up in the way you're feeling that you can start acting the same way as your significant other. It's easy to get the attitude of "well if they aren't doing it, then I'm not going to do it either", and sometimes you won't even realize it. The thing about motherhood is that it is mentally exhausting. It doesn't matter how your day went— you just know that at the end of the day, when you finally crawl into your bed, you get that glorious moment of "thank you, Lord"! You love your babies, but it's hard. Not anything anyone could have told you would or could prepare you for your new role in life, and all you can do is embrace it in all its stinky, messy, yet beautiful glory, and remind yourself that no one on this green Earth can be a better mother to your children than you.

If you are having a particularly rough day—for the love of all thing's chocolate—do NOT be afraid to ask for help! If you need just ten minutes to take a breath, do yourself a favor and politely ask your spouse. Whether it is for you to shower or go to the bathroom, or just drink a glass of wine, you deserve that small break.

After you become a parent, things will start changing between you and your spouse, and it can happen before you even notice. You no longer get the alone time you once had, the sex doesn't happen as often, and what's more, you don't even want to have sex. When you have babies crawling over you, are changing dirty diapers, wiping noses and giving all of your attention to them all day, the last thing on your mind at the end of the day is to be attentive to yet another person. That's the problem though—you tend to forget about your significant other's needs for love and affection, because you are so busy putting your all into your children.

It's not necessarily a bad thing, but over a period of time, it can cause serious strain on your relationship, and that's what you want to avoid. If you have people in your life willing to help you out as far as babysitting goes, take advantage of it. Even if it is once or twice a month, give yourself and your spouse a chance to bond without having children around. If you don't have the luxury of a babysitter, then, by all means, include your children. Go do something fun that the whole family will enjoy together, and after the little ones are down for the night, take an hour and just spend it relaxing and talking to your significant other. It might not sound like much, but alone time is important for your relationship.

Let's take a moment and discuss "postpartum depression". The importance of this is extreme, especially when you are a new mother. After you have a baby, your hormones tend to drop rather fast, and this can cause mood swings. That, and the fact that you're not sleeping well can play a significant role in your day-to-day life, and the way you treat and care for others.

It's common sense that when you don't get enough rest, you are usually cranky and sleepy all of the next day. No one can deny those feelings. We often fill ourselves with "liquid courage"—and I'm not talking about alcohol—I'm talking about caffeine. Lots and lots of coffee and energy drinks can be a reliable source to find that extra energy we need to make it through the day, but when you add children, work, exhaustion (physical and mental) and throw in a little hormonal imbalance, you can often set yourself up (not intentionally) for being a candidate of postpartum depression.

When you find yourself in a state of exhaustion, you can sometimes experience panic attacks and forgetfulness, neither of which you'd want to take place when it comes to trying to take care of a new baby.

Irritability also comes along with not getting enough sleep. Everyone tells you, "be prepared to never sleep again", and sometimes you feel like they were not kidding. Taking care of children is hard work, and yet you love it. Yes, you will get angry, and yes, you will want to walk away sometimes, but the important thing is, you don't.

You Broke Up When You Said "I Do"

During the first hours or days as a new mother, you have doctors and pediatricians telling you, "if you start getting stressed out, all you have to do is put the baby in their crib and walk out of the room. It won't hurt them to cry for a minute", and they aren't lying. When dealing with intense stress or frustration, put yourself and your baby out of harm's way. Don't feel bad if you need a minute to yourself, because it is something that every mother out there has done.
Some of the symptoms associated with PPD (postpartum depression) are:

- Doubting your ability to care for your child
- Not interested in things that were once desirable
- Feeling overwhelmed, sad, empty, or hopeless
- Difficulty concentrating or remembering details
- Feelings of anger and/or rage
- Inability to form a bond with your child
- Alienating yourself from friends or family

- Frequent thoughts about suicide or death
- Feeling inadequate, shame, guilt, or worthless
- Fatigue or extreme tiredness
- Insomnia, or you find that you are over sleeping

These are just a few symptoms to look for if you think you are experiencing postpartum depression, and if you feel you are, then do NOT be afraid to ask for help because at the end of the day, you are being responsible and strong enough to know and recognize your own needs and the need to change or get help. It's easy to get lonely once you become a mother because it seems like most of your "friends" start dropping off like flies. I would say don't take it personally, but it's hard not to. You start feeling left out, and it hurts to see all your friends going out and having fun, while you're cooped up inside taking care of kids.

If you are a part of social media, I suggest you try to find some friends with babies of their own. That way, you can start having somewhat of a social life again, and your kids can have little friends of their own. It seems scary going on social media to look for friends, but I'm not saying to go find a total stranger; instead, think about someone you went to school with. Just because you weren't friends with them then, doesn't mean you can't be friends with them now, and who knows, you might have more in common than you think.

Also, look in your area for some "mommy and me" activities. That is also a fun way to meet new people, and you can get to know one another in a safe environment. Don't let yourself get secluded and distant from your friends and family, and don't shun the idea of trying to make new friends.

If you are wanting to spend time with the people you are used to, then just invite them over to your house. It can be stressful trying to take your kids to someone else's home because your kids are forever getting into things, so make it easier on yourself, and invite some friends to your place to hang out for a while.

You Broke Up When You Said "I Do"

Learn how to become friends again with your spouse, as well. You will learn that during the years ahead of you, often times, your husband will be the only person you can fully rely on, and will be your best friend in the darkest times of your life.

It is very easy to let yourself start to feel resentment towards your significant other. As a mother, you not only endure changes physically, but mentally and emotionally too. Try not to place all of the blame on your husband's shoulders when you start feeling this way. It takes two to tango, and you knew the kind of person he was before you ever agreed to make him the father of your children (I know some situations are different, but this goes for the typical dating, finding love and/or marriage, and then have babies type of situation).

You expect to get a little bit of sympathy from your spouse and you do to some degree, but quit expecting it. You two made the decision to be together and potentially have a family, and you can't fault him for not being as worried or helpful as you are, because he doesn't have that classic "mothers' instinct", unlike you, and you have to admit that even when you do get time to yourself, you are still constantly worried that your babies aren't getting the care they deserve or that it is not good enough.

Pregnancy Brain

This is one of the worst things, besides throwing your guts up while you are pregnant, and directly after having a baby. Some people experience more severe cases than others, but it is nonetheless a pain in the rear end. The upside to this is that what you are experiencing will eventually go away and doesn't actually do any damage to your brain.

According to the director of the Women's Mood and Hormone Clinic at the University of California, San Francisco—Louann Brizendine, MD, there are fifteen to forty times more estrogen and progesterone in a woman's brain during the time she is pregnant. So, just imagine the toll that it takes on your body, and considering you don't just "bounce back" after having a baby, the side effects from being pregnant for roughly nine months can have a lasting effect on you and your body for a small time after delivery.

Taking all that into consideration and you being back in full force in taking on the task of upkeeping your household and children, write things down! Get a calendar, and for every event you have coming up, mark it. When you forget things or miss out events you were looking forward to, it can cause slight turmoil in your relationship between you being upset with yourself, and then looking to your partner to be the one that was supposed to remind you even though he might not have even known it to begin with.

Don't expect things to just go back to normal with your husband, either. Men can sometimes have hang-ups when it comes to thinking about you pushing a baby out of your private area, and it will take them time to readjust, so don't let it get you down. Accept the fact that things aren't necessarily meant to go back to the way they were before pregnancy, but you were meant to use this stepping stone in your relationship for what it is—a step in a new direction, another milestone you and your partner will take in your journey in life.

Chapter 3

"You can't change someone who doesn't want to change". You've heard the saying before over and over, but you can't seem to make it stick in your brain. "He's different", you think, "I can show him that he can be better", right?
"He will realize I'm right and he will love me more for it".

Wrong.

Ladies, your man is the exact same man he was when you first got into the relationship. You loved him then, right? People do change over time with added factors like stress and experience—it's natural, and our way of evolving to cope with our surroundings and things going on in our personal lives. That is also something that you, as an individual, do on your own, not with the constant nagging of someone else telling you that it is what you need to do.

Most people have that streak of "stubbornness" in them when they are told to do or not to do something. They will tend to do the opposite, especially if they think that there is nothing wrong with the way they are doing things.

Don't take this wrongly though. If you are in a relationship that is abusive, by all means, get out. Mental and physical abuse is not something you need to take upon yourself to try to change or much less, give in to, because most of the time, you are fighting a losing battle. Know your worth, because you deserve happiness.

When it comes to the way your spouse does things, handles themselves or bad habits they have, pick and choose your battles. There's no sense in arguing because someone forgot to take the trash out. If you have a disagreement about a larger problem like how to raise your kids, or for one of the biggest evils—

money—then do your best to really try to communicate.

Communication

One of the biggest problems in the world today is communication. People would rather ask for forgiveness instead of permission, which in turn causes for trust issues. Sure, it feels good to just yell and get all your frustration out, but if that is all you do, the lack of communication can play a big role in the demise of your relationship. Your partner isn't going to know what is wrong if you don't take time to try to explain yourself and your feelings.

High Expectations

You tend to set high expectations for yourself at a young age, envisioning the life you want for yourself and your family: The whole "white picket fence" picture, and being on the side where the grass is greener. But for grass to stay green, it has to be watered, or it will just die off. There is absolutely nothing wrong with that though—wanting the best for yourself. You just need to make sure you and your partner are on the same page when it comes to your goals in life and for yourself. Nurture the love you have for each other, and accept the fact that life happens, and every day isn't guaranteed. You will have to let things go in order to grow, because if you are constantly holding on to grudges or insecurities, you won't get anywhere—not with yourself nor your relationship.

They say that opposites attract, and that seems to be the case in most relationships, although you have to have that common ground in the middle. If you're controlling, and your spouse is laid back and easy-going, or vice versa, you have to balance each other out, and that is something only you and your significant other can figure out how to fix. No one knows you better than you know yourself.

Fix Yourself

You're so wrapped up in your partner's "flaws" and making a mental list of everything that they could change to make your life better or easier, but what about what you could do to make your own life better?

What are you unhappy about that you could possibly change on your own without having to depend on someone else to do it for you? If you are not happy with yourself, then how can you be happy with someone else?

Taking Responsibility

It is important to know and acknowledge when you have caused discomfort within the relationship and own up to it. If you go around thinking that you are always right and do no wrong, then absolutely nothing will change in your relationship. Everyone in life makes mistakes, and guess what? IT IS OKAY! What is not okay, though, is you pushing the blame on to someone else because you're afraid to look like the bad guy.

When you take responsibility for your actions, it gives you the chance to forgive yourself and learn from the experience, and in return, your partner can have the chance to forgive you and himself as well.

Vulnerability

It's also important to let yourself and your partner be vulnerable. Let yourself depend on them, and them to depend on you. Maybe not in every aspect of your lives, but you need that sense of feeling wanted or needed. Both of you do because it gives you that drive to want to make each other happy, knowing that you need them and *don't want* to lose what you have together.

Criticizing

There is a difference between complaining reasonably or expressing your feelings and criticizing your partner. Once again, communication is key when you are in a relationship. If your partner is doing something that has you in a tizzy, then calmly express your concern. For example, if your significant other gets something to eat without you, instead of shouting and saying something along the lines of, "Well that was rude, am I just not important enough for you to think about?" Insinuating that they're being selfish, try saying, "Hey, next time you're out, can you give me a call and see if I want anything, please?"

Don't lash out and try to attack their character. If you are having problems and a confrontation, it is easy to say mean things just to make yourself seem like the more intimidating person, but it is the wrong way to go. Try to avoid things like name-calling and sarcasm during an argument. Try to make a conscious effort to not get defensive when discussing things with your spouse. You have to learn to accept constructive criticism if you want things to change within your marriage or relationship. Don't expect just one of you to change, because it will take effort on both of your parts.

Like anything in life, relationships take work, tender love and care, and nurturance. It doesn't happen overnight.

Who's the Boss

When you are used to doing things your way, and you have high expectations of how your life should be, only to realize that you things might not exactly be the way you thought they would, you might find yourself fighting to take charge and making things change under your control. You will also find that it doesn't really work that way, and things will start spiraling even more out of control than what they originally were.

You are *not* the boss.

You might be the boss of your body and the boss of your life, but once others are involved, you no longer have the ability to control everything around you.

You Broke Up When You Said "I Do"

Take a deep breath and exhale – everything will be okay. Start making a conscious effort to *ask* your spouse about something *instead* of *telling* your spouse to do something. It can be as simple as taking out the trash. Instead of saying "Hey, take the trash out", change your tune and politely ask "Hey hun, would you mind taking the trash out while I start the dishes?" This way, you are getting things done in a fashionable manner, and you won't seem unappreciative or expecting.

This reasoning can take you further than just your daily household chores, but let us say you were in public somewhere, and your spouse picks up something that interests them but you think that it's nonsense, don't demand them to put it back. Instead, you should dig deep inside, don't say a word and *let it go*. You don't have to control every situation you come across. Relationships aren't a contest of who wears the pants and who doesn't; treat each other with equality.

You Broke Up When You Said "I Do"

Say What You Mean and Mean What You Say

One of the worst things when dealing with people in general is that you can't really trust their word anymore. When someone tells you that they are going to do something, you are constantly having to make phone calls and check in to make sure that they are doing just that.

When you are dealing with your significant other, the same goes. If you tell them you are going to do something, then, by all means, do it. So, when they tell you that they are going to do something, then sit tight and give them a chance to do it.

Everyone has their own way of doing things, and not everyone will do it the way you do, or the way you want them to, and it is okay. When your partner says they have things going on, but they will do whatever it is that you put on the "honey-do" list, don't nag constantly about it not getting done, and don't go and try to do something yourself just because, in your eyes, it's not being done in a timely fashion.

Not only are you doubting your spouse, but you are taking away their chance to shine and show you that they are still needed.

We all forget to do things, and it's alright if you do, as long as you communicate to each other about the situation. If you plan to fix the mess you made, then make it known and then allow time for it to get done. Remember, you both are a part of the same thing, and neither one of you want things falling down around you, so when you say you're going to do something, try to keep in mind that other people are depending on you, so be sure to uphold your end of the deal.

Chapter 4

As a parent, you want what is best for your children, in all aspects of life, careers, marriage, children it doesn't matter what it is. So, if you want all this for your children then think about what your parent would and would not want for you. More than likely the answer is that they only want what is best.

When you are struggling in your relationship, it is crucial to not divulge to others about your life and the problems you are having within your relationship. Of course, we all need that shoulder to cry on, but when it comes to discussing the details of what your partner is doing, don't go running to your mother or his. If they have siblings, you don't have to go running to them either. It's okay to have relationships with everyone on his and your side of the family, but once you start venting to them about how his attitude is mean, or how he isn't doing something right and messing things up, their (or your parents) can change their perspective of him, and if you are talking to his side of the family, they can get defensive and upset, causing their perspective of you to change.

The Parents

At the beginning of your relationship, one of the most nerve-wrecking moments is when you have to meet the "in-laws". What will they think about you? What if they don't like you or they think that you aren't good enough? What are they like? Will they be happy and easy-going, and welcome you with open arms? Are they full of judgement and think they are better than everyone else?

These are common questions we ask ourselves before meeting the parents of the person we are potentially going to spend the rest of our lives with. We try so hard to impress them, but also be who we are at the same time. We work hard on that first impression, and then continue to prove ourselves to show that we will be a suitable mate. We strive to gain that approval and to have a viable relationship with our in-laws.

If your parents are still alive and well, or if you have a great relationship with them, that's awesome. If you have a wonderful relationship with your in-laws and vice versa for your spouse, then by all means, keep it going. Just be wary of what you spill the beans about. For example, if you and your spouse are having a dry spell in the bedroom and you are feeling a little self-conscious about it and doubting yourself, maybe instead of going to your mom about what to do or express your feelings and vent, try going to a close friend of yours. When dealing with parents, they tend to get in their feelings a lot when it comes to their children. They get defensive on your part because if you are unhappy, then they hurt for you.

If your parents feel that way, imagine what his parents would feel if you start targeting their son. They will get defensive for him and maybe start thinking that *you* are the problem instead of their child, because, surely, there is a legitimate reason for their pride and joy to be feeling the way he does.

Conveying your problems with each others' parents can also cause significant friction between you and your spouse.

Once others start implementing their opinions on your relationship, you can start to agree with things they are saying and start taking their advice, but it could also be the wrong advice. Everyone, everywhere has an opinion on how things should and shouldn't be done and what is right and what is wrong, so it is best that you make those decision on your own about what you think is the right way to go about trying to manage the problems you are having. The best person to talk to at the end of the day about the things you are thinking about, however, is none other than your spouse.

Don't give in to the temptation of gossip when it comes to talking about things your husband does – good or bad.

You Broke Up When You Said "I Do"

Going beyond in-laws, let's discuss friendships and when it is acceptable to talk to friends about your relationship.

If you are going to talk about your partner, do so in a kind way. If you were to happen upon your spouse and his friends, and they were talking about how bitchy you were being, or how uptight you are, how lazy you can be, and how you do not have as much sex anymore, well, you would be livid, to say the least. So why would you want to paint your spouse in a bad image? You don't – I mean, not really. You want to be able to brag to your friends about how attentive your husband can be, and how he loves you just right; how you wouldn't know what to do without him, because he brings the very best out in you.

Do you really want people feeling sorry for you and thinking that you are in a relationship you can't seem to find the strength to get out of? Hopefully, your answer isn't yes.

You want people to look at you and your spouse, almost with envy. You should have the want to be seen as the "power couple" who can face any situation with poise and grace, and persevere through your problems instead of airing your dirty laundry for everyone to see.

When you start talking to others about your relationship, you are essentially opening yourself up for judgement. Of course, you shouldn't care what others think of you, but at the same time, you shouldn't give opportunity for further confrontation to come about.

Your friends – his too – are like "in-laws" in a sense. When you've had friends for a long time, even going back before you met your significant other, the chances of them sticking around are high. Like parents, best friends are basically a part of a packaged deal, but with both, you have to learn how and where to draw the line.

If you are being asked personal questions about your relationship, don't be shy about turning them down. A simple "I'm not comfortable talking about this topic with anyone other than _____ (insert spouses name)" will suffice. You are not obligated to divulge every detail of your life and relationship to anyone. Be respectable, and make your spouse shine in a good light, no matter what the circumstances are behind closed doors. At the end of the day, the only people who should be discussing and hashing out your own problems are none other than you and *your* lover.

Chapter 5

Freedom

Let him go, ladies.

You know how you crave your alone time – time for you alone to just unwind and let your hair down, without having to worry about trying to please someone else? Well, so does he.

First and foremost, when you are in a relationship, you have TRUST one another. Without trust, you will forever doubt the actions of the other. Second-guessing each other is such a terrifying thing, and can lead to much more than just an argument. You will develop insecurities and self-doubt, and start blaming yourself for things that are out of your control, but you feel you could've done something different to avoid it, and the list just goes on.

You Broke Up When You Said "I Do"

Assuming you have trust in your relationship, don't be afraid to let your man go out with his friends. One night, over dinner, just casually say, "You know, babe, you work hard for us and I think it would be a good idea for you to go blow off some steam and hang out with some of your friends". Let him relax and feel less pressure, and just be able to go and enjoy his time without having to worry about if he is making enough money to pay bills, or being the best him he can be. If he does go out and you are a little apprehensive, *politely* ask that he is home by a certain time, so you are not up all night worrying about him. Don't sit on the phone the whole night questioning him on where he is and what he is doing, because that will completely defeat the whole purpose of him going out.

That's all well and good, but *what about me?* Is what you are thinking right about now.

The answer to that is, *you need to do the same thing!* Don't be scared to say "Hey babe, I would really like it if you could watch the kids one afternoon or evening. I want to go to dinner with some friends and just try to relax". The door swings both ways when you are committed to someone. If you give them the benefit of the doubt on something, then they *should* be able to do the same when it comes to you and what you're doing.

Feelings

He might be "the man of the house", but trust me when I say that he, too, has feelings. We set our men up high on the pedestal of things that are "unbreakable". We expect them to be our shoulder to cry on when we need it, and they are our protectors and our providers. They should be unbreakable... Right? *NO!*

Quit being insensitive when it comes to your man being upset about something. If he comes to you with something confident or personal, *embrace it*. Most of the time men run around all "I AM MAN, HEAR ME ROAR", and that is nice most of the time, but as a woman, you more than likely want him to be

61

sensitive sometimes too, so when that moment finally arises, do not push him away or shut him down. Listen to what he has to say, because chances are, if he is talking about it, then he needs someone that will listen and not judge him.

Space

"I think we need to take a break" would probably be some of the scariest words you could ever hear when you are dating or married to someone. But why? Why is it scary to admit that you might need some time off? Why do people automatically assume that taking a break and getting some space in between you is a bad thing? It's not. If you and your spouse have been arguing like crazy and getting on each other's nerves, then, chances are, you *do* need a break.

Don't take it or mean it as "I want to break up", because the likelihood of that is slim, unless you or your partner is having an affair. But that is neither here nor there, so we're not even going to discuss it.

If you or your spouse makes the decision to take a break, then first you need to lay down some ground rules. Sit down together and talk about things that you do not want each other doing, and where you would go. Take a weekend to yourself or with just you and your kids. Whether it's just going to a hotel in town for some time, or staying a weekend with your parents and spending time with them, take the time you need to collect your thoughts and decompress. It is a lot better than staying home and arguing all weekend, and driving an even bigger wedge between the two of you.

Hobbies

Having hobbies consist of more than taking care of your kids and/or your home. We talked about giving each other space, but when you have hobbies outside of each other, then that is also a way to gain space without ever hurting each other's feelings. What are things you like to do? If bowling is your thing, then join a bowling league, or go play bingo one night a week. If the hubby likes football, then maybe he can join a fantasy team or the men's league.

Find things outside of each other that you enjoy doing that will also give you a break from your daily duties. Make them on opposite nights, so you aren't constantly trying to find a babysitter. That way, you both will be sharing the responsibility of taking care of the children (this is if you have children).

When it comes to hobbies that you enjoy doing together, absolutely indulge! There is nothing better than enjoying your time together and having fun, but you also need to let each other have the chance to enjoy things by yourselves. You might be the center of their world, but don't let it fully revolve around you.

Who Carries the Biggest Load

It does not matter who does more around the house, who works more, or who takes care of the bills, etc. Quit comparing yourself to him and try to make it seem like what you do is more strenuous, or what he does is more so. You both are carrying a different weight on your shoulders, and if you are doing your part to help him, share the responsibilities of this life you have made together – that is all that really matters.

If he works and makes enough money so you can stay home, let him do just that, and you can do your part of the bargain. There is nothing wrong with letting someone take care of you and let yourself depend on them. There is a difference between making that decision together and then taking advantage of it.

If you have children, yes, it is hard to be home and tend to their every need, only to have your significant other come home and you feel obligated to tend to them – but take into consideration what he gets up and does every day just so you can stay home and enjoy the time you have with your children.

Everyone's stress is different, so don't compare your situation to his and don't let him compare his situation to yours, because you both are playing a role in the life you have created for yourselves.

You Broke Up When You Said "I Do"

If you think that you are caging your spouse in, then start looking for ways that he could be coping. No matter what, men, and possibly yourself, will crave freedom to some degree. It is human nature, and we don't want to feel like we are trapped or have to ask permission to go and do something. If you notice that your significant other is starting to pick up habits like watching pornography or masturbating, drinking excessively, trying to get out of the house by finding a new hobby (within reason and without talking it over with you) or you start to notice that he is becoming more distracted and making himself distant, then you need to first sit down with yourself and come up with a plan, and then sit him down and have a discussion. You need to find yourselves and become happy together again, learn to love again, and remember that you are not in this relationship to control him.

This will be a difficult moment in your relationship, but do your best to remember that is just that – a moment. It does not define you or your relationship, and you have the ability to change it if you want it bad enough. It is an enlightening moment when you know that you and your partner can go out and have fun separately, and still come home knowing that you both had a good time and were able to trust each other to do so. When you give your spouse freedom, you also give yourself that same freedom to be able to enjoy yourself and do the things you want to do without him. It is okay to do things without each other, so don't be petrified by extending or having a little freedom.

Chapter 6

Is it worth it? At the end of the day when everything is said and done, is the fight you are having worth the trouble it is causing?

You always hear the saying, "Don't go to bed angry", and if you speak to any "old timers", most of them will tell you that is one of the key secrets to a successful and long-lasting marriage. There are a couple of reasons to back up the statement as well.

You Never Know What Is Going to Happen

You hear a lot of people saying that if they could choose a way to die, then it would be at night when they are asleep, and that is reason number one as to why you don't go to bed mad at each other.

You don't know what is going to happen during those long hours of the night – no one does. That is the point though. If you were to go to bed angry, only to wake up and find out you lost that person, that's not a feeling that anyone wants to experience. Is any argument you have that important?

Even when you argue during the day, don't let it ruin your day. You and your partner need to take time and talk it out so it doesn't linger. If you can't talk about it right then and there, make plans to discuss it once you get home where you are in a comfortable environment, but try not to let it linger throughout the day by being so mad at each other that you don't even want to talk, because, once again, you never know what could happen. Car wrecks and other freak accidents occur every day, and if it happens to you or someone you love, then you don't want the sting of regret or guilt hanging around.

Grudges

There is no point in holding a grudge. When you hold onto something that someone did or has said, then over time, it only makes you bitter. Be open-minded, and learn how to forgive. Remind yourself that not everyone in the world is perfect. Our lives aren't black and white, but they are filled with so many colors, so we should learn to embrace them. Just because a person has messed up or has said something out of spite, it doesn't make them a bad person not worthy of forgiveness. Give yourself a chance to change your perspective about something, or learn from others actions.

When you have been arguing on and on and you see that you're getting nowhere, now would be a good time to just stop and just ask yourself "Is it worth it?" On a scale of one to ten, how detrimental is that argument to your relationship?

It does not matter if you don't agree with each other, because, guess what? You are *not* going to agree on everything. It just isn't going to happen, and you have to understand and accept that. What a world it would be if everyone just agreed with each other! What matters is that you respect each other on the things that you disagree on. You don't have to like it, but that is your partner, your lover and your friend; it is your job to support them in their decisions, just as you expect them to support you in yours.

Make sure you always tell them you love them. The "I love you" seems so simple, but those three words are a reminder of why you are with this person. Love is hard and it takes work, dedication, blood, sweat and tears, but it is so worth it if you can get past your problems. You don't just run away when things get hard, because then you would never grow together. A simple touch when you are tucked into bed at night can make all the difference in the world when you are you fighting. It isn't like you lost the love for each other over this one argument, so you need to do your best and remember that when you find yourself so angry you don't even want to look at them. Ask yourself, "Was this fight really worth this?"

I'm not saying to forget the fight if it is something that is important to you, but be open to new ideas and reasonings. We're often so focused on trying to get our point across, or trying to make the other person see our side of things that we can sometimes be overbearing in our confrontations. It doesn't matter who gets the last word when you are fighting, as long as you both walk away with a better understanding of the other. Stubbornness can work in both directions in life, and that's either good or bad. Don't be so stubborn that you completely disregard others' feelings, but be stubborn enough that you can accomplish the things you need to do.

During every argument or misunderstanding, stop and ask yourself if it is worth it. If you think to yourself, "no", then *let it go*. You are going to continue to have disagreements for the rest of your time on this Earth. You are going to endure things that you don't want to, and have feelings that tear your insides apart; you are going to be dealing with things that, in the big scheme of things, actually matter. If you are not being hurt physically, *let it go*. If it doesn't go against your morals and personal beliefs, then *let it go*.

Make Love, Not War

Your bedroom should be a sacred place, not one where you fight and argue. You know how people tell you to leave your problems at the office? Well – leave your problems at the bedroom door.

It is common these days to find that several couples have decided to skip putting up that big flat screen TV on the wall. Although there is nothing more relaxing than crawling up in bed, under the covers and watching your favorite TV show, many believe that the bedroom is not the place for it. Make your bedroom the ultimate space for you and your spouse to love one another. When you opt to leave the TV out of your room, it almost forces you to pay attention to each other. It allows you to be able to have an actual intimate conversation with your significant other, and gives you a chance to tell secrets and laugh with each other in the dark of the night.

It also allows you to have a physical relationship with one another. Open up and find your sexuality, and explore all your options inside the bedroom.

The bedroom can make for a great "safe place". Do you remember when you were younger, and your parents would yell at you or put you on restriction, and the first place you would run to is your room, where you would continue your sulking and reevaluating of your life? Even as an adult, your bedroom can be used at your sanctuary to regain a clear mind, and can also be a place to let all your tears and fears out.

This is also the place where, ultimately, you rest. At the end of a long day, the thing you more than likely want to do is go to bed. You want peace and quiet, somewhere where you aren't bothered while you do your daily routine of showering, getting dressed, brushing your teeth and using the bathroom. Overall, your bedroom should be *your* space and yours only.

You Broke Up When You Said "I Do"

Which brings us to another point: Many people don't allow their children in their bedrooms. They don't allow their doors to always be open and let their children come and go as they please (I am not talking about not welcoming your kids into your home – just your bedroom). To each their own, and do whatever it is that you feel most comfortable with, but keep in mind that your children have their own space they can inhibit, and try to keep the constant traffic out of your area.

When confrontation arises close to that golden hour of being able to go to bed, that is another reason to leave the problems at the door, because when you've been fighting, your brain goes into overdrive and starts thinking about everything, especially that pertaining to your argument. When your brain is constantly spinning and you are trying to go sleep, what do you think happens?

You Broke Up When You Said "I Do"

You don't sleep is what happens! When you don't sleep, how do you feel? Cranky! And once again, you are on a downhill spiral to despair, and you are going to be doing everything you can to stop yourself from going there.

This might be a lot to take in all at once, and it isn't going to change overnight. It is going to take dedication, and you are going to have to persevere. Anything is possible when you put your mind to it, that your relationship with the person you love is most important.

Be sure to remember that before trying to carry an argument overnight, and ask yourself "Is it really worth it"?

Chapter 7

Equality

Do you feel inferior or not on the same level as your significant other? Do you make them feel that way? If you are walking around trying to make yourself seem like you are better than your partner, or somehow, like you deserve better, then why are you even with them in the first place?

When you are in a relationship, you have to be equal no matter what. I'm not talking about doing the same number of chores or making equal amounts of money – I'm talking spiritually, mentally and emotionally.

You have got to look at your partner and think, "I know he is in this just as much as I am", and you have to believe it. You can't think that you are the only one that puts forth the effort, and you can't think that you support him more than he does you, because if you are constantly thinking that you are better than him, how are you both going to last? Most divorces happen because one or the other is constantly thinking they are better than the other, that they are the only ones "trying" and putting more "love" into the relationship. You don't hear people divorcing because they loved equally and both put the same amount of effort into the relationship.

When you are trying to have a successful relationship, you have to establish and understand your needs. What are your needs?

Essentially, needs help you better understand who you are. If you have an introvert personality but you try to cover it up because you feel like you will be judged, and you constantly push yourself to be more outgoing or try to impress someone else and hide what your true self really needs, then you are denying yourself the chance to be *you*. It does not matter what type of personality you have, as long as YOU know what it takes to make you happy.

You Broke Up When You Said "I Do"

What do you need to make you happy? What makes you happy?

Most people don't even take the time to acknowledge their needs, but once you do, it is such an enlightening moment. You will strive to accomplish the things that you know will make you happy. If you are the type of person that is outgoing and free-spirited, and if going out every once and a while gives you the opportunity to just let go, then your partner has to understand that. The same goes for your partner too.

What do they need, and what makes them happy?

These are things that you need to establish FIRST. Recognizing what are the other's wants, needs and desires. Can you respect them on their needs?

If you don't identify your own needs, then now is the time for you to dig deep and take a look at yourself and your life and figure out what it is that you are missing. It might not happen overnight, but try to dedicate yourself to finding yourself.

You might be asking yourself right now about what any of this has to do with your man having dignity and respect, and I'm going to tell you:

Number one, if you can't recognize your own needs, then how is your partner going to recognize them? You will be swimming in a pool of unhappiness, because you are constantly let down and you can't even give a reason as to why.

Number two, if you don't know your partner's needs, then how are you supposed to make them happy and satisfy them?

If you both are unhappy all the time because you are constantly letting each other down and not satisfying each other, then how do you expect to respect your man and have him respect you? When you have the feeling that you aren't good enough, it leaves you feeling depressed, insecure and undignified. No one wants to feel like that, ever – it only leads to trouble.

After you and your partner have come to terms on what each of your needs are, the next step is to figure out what the needs of your relationship are. You both need to have a clear understanding of what it will take to be able to make your relationship a successful one.

Saying Yes

When you and your partner are having a discussion on something and trying to come to an agreement, don't just say "yes" because you are ready for the conversation to end. When saying "yes", you need to be able to do so on four different levels:

Spiritually

How the heck are you supposed to say "yes" spiritually?

You make sure that it doesn't go against your wants and needs – that's how. Often times, we can find ourselves putting others' needs before our own, and all of our desires get pushed to the back burner because we have that natural "people pleaser" personality. When you do this consistently, you tend to lose sight of yourself, and you no longer know where you are going in life because you have been so focused on making others happy that you forget to make yourself happy.

Mentally

As you grow older, you start to realize that life is exactly like "a box of chocolates" and you definitely don't know what you're getting. Nothing in life is ever the same, and you have things thrown at you all the time that makes it hard to handle, but on occasion, there will be several things that we have the opportunity to control. If something comes up and you already have a lot going on, don't say "yes" for the sake of saying it. If you know that you have too much going on or are in a tough spot in life and saying "yes" means you will be even more stressed out later on, then do *not* say it.

Emotionally

If saying "yes" makes you feel guilty, angry, or anything but happy and content, then you don't need to say it. Bottom line – don't say it if you know that the actions will cause you to get your feelings hurt later down the road. That only creates more problems and arguments later down the road.

Physically

Are you putting yourself in harms way by answering "yes"? If you think that you have no control in your life, just know that one thing for certain is that you do have control over your body and what happens to it. Do not ever say "yes" to something that you know can have the potential to cause you physical harm.

Respect and Dignity

First, let's make sure you understand the meaning of R.E.S.P.E.C.T.

The Oxford Dictionary states that respect is "a feeling of deep admiration for someone or something, elicited by their abilities, qualities or achievements". That being said, when you look at your husband or significant other, what do you feel? Are you proud of them, or ashamed? Sometimes, it is hard to admit the truth because you keep yourself "inside the box" – because you are afraid to step out of your comfort zone. If this is not the case for you and you have those feelings of respect for your spouse, then here are some things you can do to show them the respect they deserve:

First, start by giving him a kiss before he walks out of the door in the morning, and every afternoon when he returns home. It's a small way of letting him know you are thinking about him.

If you are sitting down for dinner or when he first gets home, ask him how his day was, and *look him in the eyes.* This is "killing two birds with one stone", you could say. You are showing him that you care by asking and also letting him know that he has your full attention, and you are actually listening to him.

Tell him "thank you". It doesn't matter if it is for something small that he has done or something big. Everyone likes to feel appreciated and noticed when they do something.

You Broke Up When You Said "I Do"

When you are trying to make a tough decision, even if you don't think you need his opinion, ask him anyway.

If you decide to go out to dinner or just out on the town, start by dressing up. Show him that he is worth the effort of you getting all "dolled up".

We talked about criticizing, and it is crucial that you don't criticize him in a negative way and NEVER do it in front of people. If something happens while you are out together, then either let it go or save it for home when you can talk like the adults that you are.

Don't shoot him down in the bedroom. If he wants to try something new then let him – you might actually enjoy it.

After a long day at work, let him come home to one of his favorite dinners and desserts.

You Broke Up When You Said "I Do"

Tell him that you enjoy the life you have with him and you love what you have made and accomplished together.

Men like to feel... Well, manly. If you are piddling around the house and there is something up high you need to get, ask him to come over and help you.

It's easy to find the flaws in people, so instead of doing that, start focusing on what he's doing right, and compliment him often.

If you disagree with his opinions, then do it in a kind way, and take time to understand why he feels the way he does about something.

If you have certain things coming up during the week, let him know. Don't catch him off guard and last minute to where he can't plan to participate, and lead to both you being let down.

You Broke Up When You Said "I Do"

Be happy when he is around! He is gone all day, and the last thing he wants is to come home to his wife having a bad attitude.

Write him a sweet note and leave it in his car or send him a cute text during the day just to put a smile on his face.

I know that sometimes you have a lot of things going on, especially if you have kids, but try your best to go to sleep when he does, and when he wakes up in the morning, then you get up too.

When he messes up something, be forgiving and patient. We all make mistakes, and you would be upset if he attacked you for messing up.

Don't blow his money away! He works hard to provide for his family and to pay bills, so respect it and spend it wisely on essentials. If you want to splurge, then splurge together, or ask him before going and spoiling yourself.

Do not flaunt yourself in front of other men! Wear respectable but sexy clothing for him and *him* only.

Earn his trust by keeping what he tells you a secret. If he confides in you, then don't disrespect him by going and telling your closest friends about it and making it a topic for discussion.

Ask him for his opinion on what he would like to do. If the weekend is coming up, then sit down together and ask him what he thinks would be fun.

When he succeeds in something, whether it is a personal goal or in his career, congratulate him and celebrate with him. His successes are yours too.

You Broke Up When You Said "I Do"

Last but not least – and most importantly – you need to always tell him that you love him. Always. Even if you are aggravated and upset.

When you respect someone, you are, in turn, treating them with *dignity*. The two basically go hand-in-hand with each other. If you have lack of respect for someone, then how are you going to be able to treat them with dignity? To be worthy of respect is, in itself, the definition of dignity. If you and your partner have a clear understanding of each other and your needs and you do your best to do your part in the relationship, then respecting each other will come easy. The last thing you want is to be out in public arguing because you can't agree, or one of you said something out of line.

You want to feel confident around each other and know that when you go out, you feel secure enough to know that you are doing everything you can to respect and love your partner.

You Broke Up When You Said "I Do"

Chapter 8

Sex, or the lack thereof after marriage, or when you have been together for a long time, is kind of a big deal... Or is it not?

The answer is: Yes, it is a *very* big deal. The lack of sex can straight up make you angry and just plain irritable, where sometimes, you don't even want to be around yourself. Even if you "take care of business" on your own, there is nothing like the actual act itself.

During a 1994 study conducted by the University of Chicago, it was calculated that eighty percent of married couples reported they had sex a few times a month, and thirty-two percent stated that they had sex two to three times a week! The word "few" lies somewhere between a couple (two) and several (many), so more than two times, but maybe not quite seven... Or eight? If you were to break it down and average it out, that's about two to three times a week for a month, so, it's not bad, right? Let's be honest here, though – it sometimes doesn't happen that way for some of us, and at the end of the day, it gets us down.

The feelings that come along with not having sex are probably one of the worst to have. Feeling unwanted and not deserving of intimacy are things no one should have to experience, but unfortunately, many do. You hear people saying so often, "If he isn't shacking up with you, then he must be shacking up with someone else", and it's those words of doubt that tend to push us to our lowest points. Just because you and your partner aren't putting your bodies to good use, it *does not* mean that one of you is having an affair!

You Broke Up When You Said "I Do"

We sometimes just get tired – tired of getting up and go to work, working all day, coming home, cleaning our houses, cooking dinner, running kids to and from school – and those are just normal daily activities. Never mind if life throws you a curve ball and you are having to deal with health issues of a family member or your spouse. At the end of most days, you are too tired, and sex is the last thing you will be thinking about. I mean, sure, you want to put that bed of yours to use, but not in the hot, sweaty, naked "twister" way.

The way men look at sex and the way women look at it are completely different. As women, we are emotional by nature. We tend to wear our hearts on our sleeve already, and sex can almost be added to the list of things "to do". For men, some experts state that sex is one way a man can show his emotions, since in their day-to-day life, they tend to not show as much emotion as women.

You Broke Up When You Said "I Do"

Women already put a significant amount of emotion into a lot of things like raising children, and that can oftentimes put a damper on the nightly shakedown in the sheets. If we have had a rough day, it's easier to cry it out than to keep it all bottled in, and for men, if they have had a particularly rough day, they would have to have an outlet to channel those emotions, so they would most likely lean towards sex.

If you see that you and your partner have reached that dreadful rut in your relationship, then maybe some of these tips can help you pull yourself and your spouse out of it.

My number one suggestion would be to get a "boudoir photo shoot".

What's that you ask? Well the word "boudoir" is French, and refers to a woman's bedroom or dressing area.

You Broke Up When You Said "I Do"

So, your interest is piqued now? Good. Putting two-and-two together, photo shoot and bedroom – and no, I'm not suggesting making pornography, but subtle and sexy photos of yourself that you can surprise your significant other with.

These photos have a tendency to really capture the sensuality of a woman, and that woman can be you. Once you see yourself in these photos, you will have a definite confidence boost and that, my dear, is never a bad thing when you are talking about sex with your one true love.

So where do you find someone to take these photos? That's an easy one – you just look in your town. Who do you know that is a photographer, and if you can think of any, it's just as easy to look up photographers in your area. Get on the phone and start finding out about the services provided in the city closest to you!

You Broke Up When You Said "I Do"

You might start having second thoughts once you get the ball rolling on this one, but take a chance and step outside of your comfort zone.

Before we go further, keep in mind that just because you have more sex, that doesn't mean that the sex you're having will be good. You have to have the desire to please your lover and to satisfy their sexual needs along with your own. If the sex is good or, heck, better than good, chances are, your marriage or relationship will be better.

It's also no lie that when you see your man cleaning, it does something to your insides and gets your heart all "a flutter". Seeing your partner being a dad and watching him experience the best parts of life can also give you that giddy feeling, so it should come as no surprise that when you share responsibilities with your partner and they help out as much as they can, you would be more willing to jump in the sack.

With that comes the next suggestion:

Kids – sure, they are cute and cuddly, but they are bad for your sex life. If you are trying to get down and dirty, they do not need to be around. The further away they are, the better.

Take an evening and get the kids out of the house – like for the *whole night*. Without you. Send them to grandma's house, your sibling's house, or to a friend's house – it doesn't really matter. Just get them out.

You and your spouse are then about to have a "sex-athon".

Go buy the latest book on sexual positions, eat dinner so you can keep your strength, turn the lights down low and get between the sheets or on the table – whatever and wherever your heart desires. Just go do it, for God's sake!

You Broke Up When You Said "I Do"

Sex can be tiring, and if you aren't used to doing it all the time, this suggestion might come with some difficulty. Spice it up some and spread it out throughout an entire weekend. When it comes to sex, all you need to say is "YES" – and I do mean it in more than one way.

It's no secret that things change once you settle down and gain responsibilities, have children, and so on. Don't be scared of the changes, though, because that's what we do – we learn to adapt and evolve to suit our current habitats and situations.

The next suggestion is to just talk with your partner – open your heart and ears up to have an intimate conversation. Find ways to reconnect by using your words, feelings and imagination, and you would be surprised at the opportunities for great sex that it brings.

Sex is a natural thing not only to experience, but also to want or need, and you will be forever chasing that euphoric feeling that it brings you when you are finally with your partner. If you can't be open and honest about what it takes to make you all hot and bothered, then you *will* be let down when it comes to playing in the bedroom. So, talk often with each other and find out what you want and what your expectations are when it comes to sex – you both will appreciate it.

Coming back to suggestions, have you ever thought about hiring a sex coach?

One of perks of hiring a sex coach is that they can offer you a different perspective. There's that "thinking outside of the box thing" again. They are also a great resource for tips and tools to use inside and outside of the bedroom, and can offer insight to the more technical side of sex that you or your partner might not even think about. They can oftentimes offer you more information than you can get by reading a book – but at least now you know that it is an option – one that I should say, you shouldn't be embarrassed about, but look at it as a new adventure for you and your lover.

Another thing you can do is talk dirty – that's right, turn that pretty, sophisticated mouth into a naughty dream land.

Most of the time, talking dirty makes people uncomfortable, but you won't ever know it unless you try it out. It's something about hearing those filthy words that can put that little "zing" in your belly.

If you and your partner try it and realize that it is not for you, then there's no harm done. Take it as a learning experience, and mark it off the list of things that you have done.

Some people say that watching porn together can be a good way to get in the mood to do the deed, and then there are some that say don't do it. Once again, do what you are comfortable.

If you decide that you want to give it a try, it can be a source of getting new ideas or new positions you want to try that you otherwise wouldn't think about.

Sex toys.

There's something naughty about just thinking of using sex toys with your partner. Sometimes, there are also insecurities that come along with using them. The thing about sex toys is that sometimes, they are made to give you different sensations. You will experience different things than what you would if you were just flesh-to-flesh with your partner, and that's okay – they are made to be different. If your partner experiences hesitation, then do your best to reassure them that it will be fun, and on the off chance that it's not, no one is forcing you to keep using them. However, if you both enjoy them and have fun, well then, you can both now look forward to using the "dirty little secret" in the future.

The next suggestion can be perceived as a little taboo when it comes to having an audience.

Masturbation is usually something done when no one else is watching, but if you are looking to spice up your sex life with your spouse, then this can definitely be used as an ingredient.

Not only can masturbation relieve stress and alter your mood (in a good way), it has the ability to let you be vulnerable if you're doing it in front of your partner. When you make the decision to let your partner watch you, it can heighten the intimacy and give your partner a chance to watch you feel good. Use this suggestion as foreplay when it comes to getting ready for the final act.

You Broke Up When You Said "I Do"

We talked about having kids and how women sometimes put sex on the backburner. That statement holds true, especially when sometimes, the wife has the lower sex drive. Hormones and stress can do that to a girl; but when you recognize that about yourself, then start putting sex at the top of the list when it comes to priorities. Why?

Think about what you are missing! The toe-curling, breath-catching moment when two become one! Not only that, but as a couple, your relationship depends on it just for the sole fact that without it, feelings get hurt. Don't let your spouse feel like they are undesirable.

If you are having a dip in your sexual drive, don't be scared to go to the doctor's and get it checked out. You aren't crazy, but you could have hormonal imbalances – that often happens after having children, or during the years of menopause.

You Broke Up When You Said "I Do"

If your partner is adamant about sex – or even if they aren't – just do it! You might not be in the mood now, but hopefully, after spending several minutes in a compromising position with your partner, all your inhibitions will be set free and you will be "in the mood".

Conclusion

Congratulations! You made it through to the end of *You Broke Up When You Said 'I Do': How to make your husband the happiest person in the world by changing these behavioral habits that women develop in long-lasting relationships.* While reading this book, I hope you found all the tips and tools provided most helpful when it comes to putting life back into your marriage.

Throughout the duration of this book, you should have learned how to let yourself and your spouse have some freedom, and recognized the importance of keeping your relationship private when it comes to friends and family.

Using these tips, realize the importance of learning about yourself and your needs, and how it can, in turn, help you learn your partner's needs. Respecting yourself can be hard sometimes, but the outcome of it is so beautiful – especially when you can open your heart and arms to your loved one.

"When the going get's tough, the tough gets going" – after you have completed this book, you should be able to somewhat understand the dedication it takes to making a change within your marriage, and that all good things come to those who work hard for it. Marriage and relationships are no walk in the park sometimes, and if you are in it for the long haul, then you will have to persevere through the wind and the rain to be able to see the sun on the other side.

Once again, thank you for taking the time to read the book, and hopefully, you enjoyed it as much as I did writing it!

Connect with us on our Facebook page

www.facebook.com/bluesourceandfriends and stay

tuned to our latest book promotions and free

giveaways.

Lightning Source UK Ltd.
Milton Keynes UK
UKHW011126051220
374629UK00002B/437

9 781702 999779